CURIO NO. 1

THE AVOCADO TOAST MANIFESTO

A MILLENNIAL SURVIVAL GUIDE

ABIGAIL F. BROWN

CIDER MILL PRESS

BOOK
PUBLISHERS
KENNEBUNKPORT, MAINE

13-Digit ISBN: 978-1-60433-856-0
10-Digit ISBN: 1-60433-856-3

This book may be ordered by mail from the publisher. Please include $5.99 for
postage and handling. Please support your local bookseller first!

Books published by Cider Mill Press Book Publishers are available at special
discounts for bulk purchases in the United States by corporations, institutions, and
other organizations. For more information, please contact the publisher.

Cider Mill Press Book Publishers
"Where good books are ready for press"
PO Box 454
12 Spring Street
Kennebunkport, Maine 04046
Visit us online!
www.cidermillpress.com

Typography: Rival

Printed in China
1 2 3 4 5 6 7 8 9 0
First Edition

CONTENTS

"

BOOMER:

How did you get in
this position?

MILLENNIAL:

By doing every single thing
you told me to.*

*This is a clapback. If you don't know what a
clapback is, look it up.

MILLENNIALS ARE KILLING THE INTRODUCTION

YOU'RE A MILLENNIAL. You've been blamed for your fair share of world tragedies. If media outlets are to be believed, you've single-handedly killed napkins, diamonds, fabric softeners, marriage, and forced thousands of JCPenney and Toys"R"Us employees out of a job. Way to go, you monster.

This handbook is full of ammunition against all your critics, with a fair share of facts thrown in. So, whether you're on your way to one of your three full-time jobs or sitting down to enjoy overpriced avocado toast (which is why you can't buy a house, obviously), this book is your friend. Filled with twice the facts of a clickbait article and more authentic than the Kardashians, this handbook is your first line of defense against the army of baby boomers, naysayers, and spray-tanned politicians who blame you for absolutely everything. You might be surprised how much is actually not your fault, and how the gripes directed at your generation aren't so different from those that your parents' and grandparents' generations had to shoulder.

Remember, most of the conversations in this book are opinions, and you know what they say about opinions: everyone's got one. But millennials need a safe space for theirs. The dialogues in this book are part satire, part witty clapback, and part painful truth. If you end up learning something from this book, try not to blame us. We don't need you killing the publishing industry as well.

WHO ARE MILLENNIALS?

Millennials get a bad rap. They've been called lazy, entitled, tradition-destroying, and selfish. They are individualists who can't accomplish anything without the influence of their peers and who are more obsessed with taking selfies and picking the right hashtag than saving for their future or keeping corporations afloat. At least, that's what they've been told over and over again by everyone from the media to their aunt

Linda, who doesn't understand why they can't just get married and buy a house already. But what exactly is a millennial?

The term "millennial" was first coined in 1991 in the book *Generations* by Neil Howe and William Strauss; they used it to describe the generation that started around 1981 and ended, . . . well, people can't really agree when the millennial generation technically closed. Some say 1995 was the cutoff for millennials, ushering in the age of "Gen Z" and their surrealist humor. Others push the ending of the millennials forward another five years, creating a generation that ranges from 38-year-old adults to teens who graduated high school in 2018. Named the "Me Me Me Generation" by *Time* magazine, millennials get blamed for most of the changing economic and social climate in the United States and around the world, with good reason. The millennial generation is larger than even the baby boomers (we'll get back to them in a second) and has the potential to completely change the established economic and political spheres. While not necessarily unified on any one front, millennials are, without really intending to, already causing a huge shift in the way the world runs. From preferring take-out meals over home-cooked food to delaying the purchase of a home and living with their parents well into their 30s, this generation seems nothing like the generations that came before them, a departure that terrifies both economists and baby boomers.

But millennials were also born into a rapidly changing and developing world. Barely through their first year of college (or life, if the 2000 cutoff date applies) when 9/11 shook the United States to its core and ignited the War on Terror, millennials have lived with instability since their first words. They watched technology develop from the car phone to the smartphone. They listened to cassettes, CDs, MP3s, and fell into the world of online music streaming long before they finished high school. They have experienced VHS tapes, DVDs, Blu-rays, and the rise of Netflix. They watched the 2008 recession hit and have lived through more official wars than many of the generations before them, all while barely in their teens. For the generation who gets hit with revolutionary technology every six months and barely has time to breathe between national and global emergencies, the stability of the baby boomers seems like a pipe dream.

But we've mentioned the baby boomers at least three times now, so we should probably talk about them before they call our managers to complain.

WHO ARE THE BABY BOOMERS?

Baby boomers are the good ol' generation of the past. Named for the sudden boom in population following the end of Word War II, this generation was born between 1946 and 1964 and accounts for one of the largest population spikes in American history. They protested the draft, preached peace, love, and happiness, and are one of the most financially successful generations ever, holding 80% of U.S. net worth

BOOMER:

You act like the internet
is a refuge.

MILLENNIAL:

It's the only place I can produce the fantasy you've been comfortably living in for half a century.

and, until recently, purchasing a majority of consumer goods (a position that millennials are slowly edging them out of). They grew up in the days before seat belts, ran behind the DDT van in the summers, and were one of the last groups to benefit from low-cost, debt-free higher education. They bought their first house at 29 on average and solidified the American Dream as the standard of living for the nuclear family.

They are also painted as the generation most critical of millennials and are responsible for the creation of the #howtoconfuseamillennial trend on Twitter (which immediately turned against them, predictably enough). Projected to live longer than any generation before them, many baby boomers are still in the workforce long past their 60s, holding jobs in upper management and ownership positions.

Accosted by many as being the "Selfish" and the "Mine Mine Mine Generation" (sound familiar?) they have been blamed for aggressive corporate policies, fiscal irresponsibility, and overwhelming greed, not to mention a large chunk of the carbon emissions that cause global warming.

Huh, it's almost like Americans, and humans in general, like blaming one generation for the problems of another. Weird how that works out.

On the flip side of the financial seesaw (which we banned for safety reasons after this generation grew up), the baby boomers are woefully unprepared for retirement. Only about 40% of them have invested in a retirement fund, and of that 40% many aren't sure their money will last. With their life span projected at 80 to 85 years on average (almost 10 years longer than the generation before them), their pensions and Social Security stash may start to run thin. And let's not forget the changes the baby boomers have lived through: 1955 is a world away from 2018. This groovy generation was around for the founding of Microsoft, and watched computers, legislation, and inflation change the job market from a firm handshake and a well-tailored suit to a veritable war zone rife with unemployment and minimal benefits. They were still around when segregation was the norm (and fought against it during the civil rights movement) and raised their kids during the heated conclusion of the Cold War up through the start of the War on Terror. The lifetime of the baby boomers has been far from quiet and ideal, but that doesn't change the fact that they've enjoyed more financial security, and excess, than the generations that have come after them.

AS A
GENERATIONAL
RULE

WE'VE BEEN tossing out generation names quicker than a 2008 mortgage lender doling out foreclosure notices, so we might as well list some concrete time stamps to go with them. Here are the boxes statisticians stick you in depending on what loop around the sun you got kicked off on. It's not our fault they have such weird names.

GI or Greatest Generation
Born: 1901 to 1924
Shaping Events: Great Depression, WWII
Just the Facts: This generation gained their name by overcoming the challenges of their time. The Roaring Twenties gave way to this stoic, unapproachable, and determined generation that fixed what broke and got rid of what couldn't be fixed—which explains why they ditched Herbert Hoover.

Silent Generation
Born: 1925 to 1942
Shaping Events: Economic Upswing, McCarthyism/Second Red Scare
Just the Facts: Born just before, during, or just after the Great Depression, this generation gained their name for their conformance to the status quo. Thanks to McCarthy-era witch hunts and general paranoia, this generation stayed largely quiet about social change and instead buckled down and worked on their careers. The Second Red Scare kept this generation in the black.

Baby Boomers
Born: 1946 to 1964
Shaping Events: Vietnam War Protests, Woodstock, Kennedy Assassination, Cold War
Just the Facts: The largest generation until the birth of millennials, this generation lived through political and cultural upheaval and settled into relative financial prosperity after college. Reckless, selfish, and free-spirited, this generation earned the title of "Mine Mine Mine Generation."

Gen X
Born: 1965 to 1979
Shaping Events: Latchkey Kids, MTV, AIDS Epidemic, Rise of the Internet
Just the Facts: Also known as the forgotten generation, Gen X watched technology advance at an incredible pace, all in the shadow of the baby boomers and then the millennials. They may get their time in the spotlight eventually, if they don't get trampled by Gen Z.

Millennials or Gen Y
Born: 1980 to 1995
Shaping Events: Climate Change, Columbine High School Massacre, 9/11, War on Terror, Sandy Hook Elementary School Shooting, Social Media, Barack Obama, #MeToo
Just the Facts: Named the "Me Me Me Generation" or the "Selfie Generation" by *Time* magazine, millennials are the first generation to fully embrace social media and the internet. millennials put their priorities above tradition, undermining the corporate, political, and societal status quo—all while eating a surprising number of avocados.

Gen Z or iGen
Born: 1996 to 2005
Shaping Events: The Marjory Stoneman Douglas High School Shooting, Marriage Equality, Ferguson Riots, Women's March, March for Our Lives
Just the Facts: Gen Z is known for its surrealist and nihilistic humor, blunt language, and their rejection of gender norms. Born during the War on Terror, members of Gen Z have seen more national division in their lifetime than most of the generations before them—and they have no qualms tweeting about it.

So that's the gist of it. Now that you have a lay of the land, let's jump into the real purpose of this book: arguments. Okay, the purpose of this book isn't to start an argument (and we claim no responsibility for any throwdowns, verbal or otherwise, that this book starts; just make sure to record and upload them to WorldStar, for posterity's sake).

Our goal is to start a conversation about culture and cultural shifts, which are very real, but also nothing new. After all, both millennials and baby boomers live in the same world, and they share more life experiences than you'd think.

Accusations are often little more than the parroting of commonly held opinions. Our job is to arm you with the facts, no matter what "side" you're on, so you can get a better idea of the world we all share today through a smart and cutting examination of the not-too-distant past. And for the people who can't be reasoned with? Well there should be enough clapbacks in here for you to hold your own in any coffee shop, family gathering, or boardroom you might find your way into.

"

BOOMER:

Millennials can't even
spell without the internet.

MILLENNIAL:

That's because you stopped
paying our teachers.

"

"F" IN
FUNDING

AH, MIDDLE SCHOOL. A time that no one looks fondly on, not even the teachers.

If you listen to the baby boomers, they grew up during the golden days of public education. And with corporal punishment, asbestos, segregated school systems, and solid metal slides, what's not to love?

Education has always been a rocky topic in the United States, and its public school system has fallen from grace in recent years, taking a nosedive in everything from test scores to general safety compared with schools in Europe. With a mere 3% of the national budget allocated for education, it's no surprise that school systems everywhere are desperate to raise their test scores, whether that means changing the entire structure of the SAT yearly or fudging standardized test results to keep star athletes on the playing field.

The fall of the public school system can be traced back to (you guessed it) the baby boomers. With the rise of Reaganomics (see "A Taxing Subject," page 66) and massive tax cuts, the country's infrastructure was put on the Atkins diet long before millennials were born. And while the Teflon President's policies cut inflation, they increased the national deficit by 186%.

Sure, everyone accepts that the U.S. government's debt is an imaginary number at this point, but this deficit seriously impacted future infrastructure. And no, we don't just mean the potholes on the Capital Beltway. Economics 101 for everyone at home: when less of our tax money goes to the federal and state governments, less gets invested back into public works. And despite the cries from the states-rights-first crowd, local contributions can only do so much to support a school system. It's like a merry-go-round of cause and effect that ends with stressed-out teachers, second-rate supplies, and undereducated students.

Not only has the system started to tank harder than Sears, but there is a massive teacher deficit in the United States. And it's not hard to see why. Most educators go through four to eight years of schooling before their first teaching job, not to mention the ongoing rat race of new classes needed to stay at the top of their field (which they do on their own time, by the way). And thanks to the spike in college costs and debt per capita, teachers are almost guaranteed to spend a majority of their lives in debt.

Times are so hard, even the Magic School Bus was repossessed.

The only upside to the tax laws is that for the average person, taxes have actually stayed relatively the same since 1945. But without the contributions of the top percentage of Americans, the K–12 school system is likely to continue to sink.

BOOMER:

Aw, do you need a safe
space from real life?

MILLENNIAL:

No, just from
school shooters.

Violence in America is, unfortunately, nothing new. Most baby boomers can remember the University of Texas tower shooting, a sign that public education and public safety were not what they had always been. But for millennials, growing up around the time of the Columbine High School massacre, the Sandy Hook Elementary School shooting, and the Virginia Tech massacre, school is no longer a guaranteed safe space for them.

Conservative estimates place the number of mass school shootings in the United States in 2017 at over 60 incidents. That means that there were five school shootings in the United States every month in 2017.

Teachers have started running kids as young as kindergarten age through school shooting drills. While similar to the nuclear strike drills that baby boomers went through during their school years, with the current statistics, teachers are more likely to face down a rogue gunman than

Putin's missiles—though with the way politics are going, who knows.

Blaming school shootings on the fall of infrastructure is a stretch even for us, but a lack of funding (especially for security) certainly hasn't helped. Thankfully, there has been a resurgence in the push for school funding, and the outcry against low wages for hardworking teachers has never been this loud before. Hopefully, millennials will be as willing to invest in the education of future generations as they are in Starbucks coffee.

BOOMER:

I just worry that you don't have all the knowledge you need to make it in this world.

MILLENNIAL:

I can't afford to take out
any more loans based on
what you see as a lack
of knowledge.

HIGHER LOANING

Millennials are the most educated generation in American history. And with the amount of education debt hanging over their heads, they may be the last. Gen Z has had a front-row seat to their older siblings spending thousands on college only to have to move back home with Mom and Dad and work at McDonald's. An eye-opening example for American youths.

But, like most things, this isn't really the millennials' fault. Since the boomers had their glory days on America's college campuses, the cost of a bachelor's degree from public and private universities has skyrocketed. The average cost of a degree from a public college jumped 213% since the '80s, with tuition alone spiking by 150%. This isn't including the cost of books, housing, meal plans, and external fees, not to mention that getting government aid has become more and more difficult, with federal loans covering only a fraction of tuition costs.

Despite boomer complaints, millennials aren't signing their lives away for a degree in underwater basket weaving. Gone are the days of the New-Age Psychology major, and much like their political presence, millennials have broad ambitions to change the world with their education. Newly emerging fields in computer science and groundbreaking technology top the list for millennial degrees, with technical pursuits like architecture, engineering, and medical technician following closely behind. Don't count the millennials out of the business sphere either, as marketing and finance are also popular career choices.

But the biggest issue facing millennials isn't the practicality of their study of choice, it's the cost of their education. Most college degrees will take the average millennial over 10 years to pay off and run them close to $550 a month, and that's on the lower end. Community colleges are no better, with tuition hikes keeping pace percentage-wise with private institutions.

B O O M E R :

Millennials are so entitled.

MILLENNIAL:

How was going to college
for nearly free?

On top of education, millennials are facing a stagnant job market that is hesitant to invest in new talent. There's no denying that the job market is more complex than it was 20 or 30 years ago, and with an increase in qualified workers there is a decrease in the amount of wages earned in entry-level positions. In some cases, these positions are almost nonexistent as companies try to lure younger workers into unpaid internships with the promise of experience.

Will millennials eventually get out from under the giant, looming student debt cloud of doom hanging over their heads? Probably, but not before their delayed start upsets everything from the job market to politics and population growth.

Baby Boomer
Average Cost of Public College Tuition for One Year: $3,190
Average Cost of Private College Tuition for One Year: $15,160
Average Student Debt: Nearly Nonexistent
Average Annual Income Out of College: $24,306
Average Cost of Rent: $670

Verdict: Able to gain a college education with practically no debt, boomers were ahead of the game compared to millennials. In a bonus turn of events, the average college-educated millennial makes as much as a baby boomer high school graduate did. But what goes around comes around; baby boomers who cosigned on their children's student loans are now feeling the brunt of higher education costs.

Millennial
Average Cost of Public College Tuition for One Year: $9,970
Average Cost of Private College Tuition for One Year: $34,740
Average Student Debt: $40,000
Average Annual Income Out of College: $34,035
Average Cost of Rent: $1,358

Verdict: With over 63% of millennials carrying some form of college debt, life will have to wait. Most millennials have put off getting a mortgage, a car, or even having kids until they're financially stable—which may be way down the road for these cash-strapped youths. Thanks to the overwhelming pressures of student debt, millennials may hold anywhere between two and four jobs to help cover costs, and it's still not enough.

*All stats have been adjusted for inflation.

BOOMER:

You won't even work if you
don't have beanbag chairs
and a Ping-Pong table.

MILLENNIAL:

We want our workplace
to be as serious as your idea
of a livable wage.

UNDEREMPLOYMENT
FAIR

MOST MILLENNIALS entered the U.S. workplace between 1995 and 2010, with the youngest millennials filling the ranks of part-time employees at retail stores and chain restaurants across the nation. With unemployment just passing 4% in 2017, hiring trends certainly seem to favor the younger generation.

So what's the holdup?

When the baby boomers were entering the workplace between 1961 and 1979, they faced a similar majority of the past generation in the workforce. And for both generations the unemployment rate over their peak job market years averages out to about 6.2%: not fun by any stretch of the imagination, but far from the all-time United States record of 24.9% unemployment during the Great Depression.

The difference is in the rate that boomers are retiring, which for about half of them is not at all. As of 2015, they made up close to 40% of the workforce, mainly holding management positions. And that's not just the younger baby

BOOMER:

Millennials are lazy
layabouts unwilling
to work.

MILLENNIAL:

That's because you still
haven't retired.

boomers; surveys show that 18.9% of baby boomers over 65 are still working. These older workers are changing the entire workforce age average, raising it to almost 42 years old as of 2016.

For a healthy dose of perspective, when boomers had been established in the workforce for 20 years, the Silent Generation only made up about 30% of the workforce, with that dropping off to only 10% three years later.

The boomers just aren't leaving. Part of this has to do with their longer life spans. They're predicted to live almost 20 years longer than previous generations, and for many of them retirement came as an afterthought, meaning those savings are looking about as thin as their hair right about now.

But millennials may have gotten the bum end of the deal. Right as a majority of millennials were poised to enter the workplace, the U.S. market hit one of the largest recessions since the

Great Depression, which affected employment opportunities for almost four years. With major companies and small-time businesses refusing to hire new workers until the economy stabilized, many millennials couldn't find a job, setting them further down on the corporate ladder than boomers would have been at the same point in their careers.

Before you start an angry Twitter debate about why boomers should up and leave the workforce like their parents did, keep in mind that the boomer generation was the largest single generation until the millennials, and they didn't suffer the effects of WWII like their parents did, meaning it's perfectly logical that there would be more of them in the workforce overall. They're also healthier on average than their parents— most of them are at the peak of their life (and career) right now.

BOOMER:

You're not the center of everything.

MILLENNIAL:

No, just the shitstorm
your generation managed
to stir up.

,,

The Great Recession
When: 2006 to 2009, with impacts as far as 2018
Major Influences: Shadow Banking, Subprime Mortgages, Zero-Down Housing, Early 2000s Energy Crisis
Just the Facts: The Great Recession, or the 2008 recession, was one of the worst declines in American history, second only to the Great Depression. After the dot-com bubble burst in the early 2000s, investments shifted to favor property and real estate, with more people than ever investing in the housing market. With subprime mortgages and no-paper loans (loans that depend only on your credit scores) more popular than frosted tips, the economy boomed, and shadow banking flourished. With the deregulation ushered in by Ronald Reagan's fiscal policies, loans were the new savings, and banks could simply hand off unpaid loans to secondary collection agencies. When this ill-thought-out capital hit the main market, it caused a housing bubble that finally burst in 2006, leaving big banks with less in the vault

than George Bailey (that's a boomer reference, by the way; feel free to Google it). Pair those poorly researched and irresponsible loans with an energy crisis caused by soaring oil prices and you've got an economic tsunami. The overall unemployment rate (including part-time workers) hit 17.1% in October 2009 and the federal government handed out hundreds of trillions of dollars in investments to try and stabilize big banks. People defaulted on their loans, homes were foreclosed upon, and 8.7 million people were out of a job. And the market still hasn't fully recovered, as employment rates and gas prices just barely reached pre-recession levels in 2017. Hitting the oldest of millennials just as they settled into the job market and the younger ones as they were barely in their teens, the Great Recession created this generation's patented financial insecurity and overwhelming apprehension around debt, loans, and long-term employment.

"

BOOMER:

Millennials just don't
work hard enough!

MILLENNIAL:

I can't talk now, late to one
of my three full-time jobs.

Baby Boomers
Starting Employment Range: 1961 to 1985
Average Unemployment Rate: 6%
Highest Overall Rate: 10.8% in 1982
Lowest Overall Rate: 3.4% in 1968
Verdict: Boomers faced a stable job market overall during their entrance into the workforce; while there were some economic downturns, their low taxes and thriving economy allowed them financial security during their working years.

Millennials
Starting Employment Range: 1995 to 2016
Average Unemployment Rate: 6.6%
Highest Overall Rate: 9.9% in 2009
Lowest Overall Rate: 3.9% in 2000
Verdict: The 2008 recession cut off many millennials just as they were entering the job market, leading to false career starts and financial issues down the road; this economic instability also explains the rise in multiple part-time jobs due to the scarcity of long-term positions.

Rise of the Gig

Recent studies show that over 50% of millennials have a side hustle or gig to earn extra money. The leading cause: student loans and the rising cost of living. Baby boomers are taking to the internet to earn extra cash as well, with 25% finding a supplementary source of income in an area they are passionate about.

Job Hopping

Millennials show less business loyalty than boomers, spending an average of just two years at one job compared to the national average of five years. Due to the competitive job market, millennials are more likely to hop jobs to find a better source of employment.

BOOMER:

You act like your
generation has it worse
than everyone else.

MILLENNIAL:

Give it another five years,
I'm sure you'll find some
way to screw things up
for my kids.

UNREAL
ESTATE

"BOOMERANG CHILDREN" is the term for young adults who leave their parents' house, live on their own for a length of time, and then return home. Of course, not all millennials end up back with their parents, but for many the cost of housing, food, and everything else that comes with being a #adult is practically impossible to pay for on minimum wage, or an entry-level salary, for that matter. More adults are living at home with their parents than in generations past, and close to 30% of millennials rely on financial support from their parents or guardians long after they've moved out of the house.

Millennials came of age in the middle of the housing crisis. Being able to afford a basic apartment is a pipe dream, with over 32% of millennials living with their parents. For comparison, it took three years on average to earn the deposit on a home in the '80s. In 2018, that number was up to 19 years. And with entry-level jobs paying in experience instead of raises, many millennials find themselves making the choice between living in a cardboard box under the I-95 overpass or spending every evening watching *Jeopardy!* with their aging parents. I'll take Crippling Debt for $200, Alex.

Not only does this explain the drop in millennial homeowners, but it also is incredibly difficult to start a relationship when you are still living in your childhood bedroom. *You* try to be romantic with a Hannah Montana poster staring at you from the wall. We dare you.

At least they still have avocado toast to fall back on.

BOOMER:

My taxes pay for
your education.

MILLENNIAL:

And for the rest of my life,
my wages will pay for your
retirement benefits.

"

BOOMER:

It saddens me that you'll never know the joy of owning your own home.

MILLENNIAL:

It saddens me that you still think we're living in the world you inherited and spent the next four decades pillaging.

A TAXING
SUBJECT

AH, TAXES. Nothing captures the American spirit like finding legal loopholes and putting things off until the last minute. Every dollar-earning American can bond over their absolute hatred of having to pay the government a dime more than they think it's owed. Public servants of all walks of life have undoubtedly had the "my taxes pay your salary" line thrown at them from a middle-aged American on a tax-funded sidewalk breathing tax-protected clean air, and teachers spend countless hours dreaming of the day when raised taxes will finally allow them to take a vacation. No, summer break doesn't count.

As much as it pains Americans of all stripes to admit come April, taxes are an important part of the infrastructure of our country. They pay for roads, health care, defense, and Social Security, as well as the national parks and NASA.

And honestly, who can hate NASA? They just want to see the stars.

While watching a chunk of your paycheck fly out the window to Washington, D.C., every year evokes a similar feeling to the penny whistle solo from *Titanic*, even the highest grossing billionaire in the U.S. today has it easy compared to years past. During WWII, taxes on income in the highest tax bracket topped out at 94%. Yes, you read that correctly, 94%.

You can take a seat if you need to. We had to.

That's hard to imagine in any context, but in 2017, the number was 39.8%. Today, a tax rate of 94% would mean that if Bill Gates somehow earned his entire life savings again as taxable income within the highest tax bracket (take your time, progressive tax laws are confusing), under the 1945 tax laws, he would go from $98.3 billion dollars to $5.9 billion. For the rest of us, that means for every dollar earned in that highest tax bracket by the top 1%, they would get to keep six cents.

Excessive as that sounds, fighting Nazis was expensive, and speaking out against WWII did not gain you any friends in 1945. Well, maybe a few Nazis, but they didn't make the best dinner guests. The higher tax rate stayed relatively constant over the following 20 or so years, dropping back to 85% in 1951 only to swing back to a maximum tax rate of 90% in the 10 years following the birth of the boomers.

The baby boomers were born in a golden age of American infrastructure. Sure, America didn't make any real moves to pay off its national debt, because why think that far ahead, right? But the amount of money available for public projects like education, Social Security, health care, and even military spending was astronomical compared to the years following the tax cuts pushed by Ronald Reagan. In 1989, taxation hit the lowest point in recent American history, with only 25% of the top income going toward the government. Talk about a downswing.

This meant not only that the wealthiest baby boomers get to enjoy the investments of their parents before them, but they also haven't had to contribute nearly as much toward the infrastructure that their children would inherit. It's no wonder that Social Security is almost bankrupt and that the school system is creaking under its own weight. With less revenue from taxes bolstering the Great American Dream, it's starting to look like the Great American Trailer Park.

"

BOOMER:

Your generation lacks
leadership skills.

MILLENNIAL:
Just like the government
your generation runs.

"

FIGHT FOR YOUR RIGHT TO NO PARTY

MOVE OVER, baseball, it's time for America's favorite pastime: politics. From Nixon and Reagan to Bush, Obama, and Trump with some Clinton sprinkled in between, both boomers and millennials have seen their fair share of political upheaval. It's no surprise that recent statistics show that 85% of boomers and millennials distrust the government. At least they can both agree on political paranoia.

Like most young and hopeful generations before them, millennials are more liberal-leaning than their aged counterparts, while boomers hold on tightly to conservative values like their parents did. But that's where the similarities between the politics of these generations end.

In a not-so-surprising twist, millennials may be killing the bipartisan industry.

While most millennials are liberal-leaning on social issues, a larger chunk of millennials identifies as independent (44%) than with a particular party. That's a huge increase from previous generations, and the numbers keep climbing.

So what's the deal?

Millennials as a whole are less loyal to brand names than other generations. While this applies most to consumer trends, the shift from latching on to something for the sake of the name to investing in the end product applies to politics, too. Millennials' beliefs are as quick-changing and idiosyncratic as their social media accounts. For this trendy generation, the idea of being confined to one "identity" is worse than slow Wi-Fi. That means calling themselves "Democrats" or "Republicans" is even less appealing.

Will millennials actually kill the two-party system like the mainstream media fears? Probably not. Even though the surge toward Bernie Sanders during the 2016 presidential primaries showed a sharp change in young American voters' ideals, the only drastic difference millennials brought with them to the polls was their willingness to get out and vote. In the 2016 presidential election, about 54% of millennials voted, either in person or by absentee ballot, a marked 5% more than previous years. And social media platforms, including Facebook, Snapchat, and Twitter, all started voter registration campaigns for the 2018 midterm elections to help bump up voter turnout. Plus, with the rise of protests and political activism among millennials, we might be seeing a revival of political involvement on a large scale. Or we could be in for a steady mellowing of this radical generation like the baby boomers before them.

BOOMER:

You're not the only ones who care about equality and diversity. Ever heard of a little thing called the civil rights movement?

MILLENNIAL:

Mm-hm, and you all
kept going until even
corporations were
seen as people.

TUNE IN, TURN UP, SPEAK OUT

NOW THAT we've convinced you that the total failure of the United States' economic, societal, and political systems is imminent, let's get serious for a moment. Sure, humanity sucks big time, especially compared to kittens on the internet, but we've come a long way. Thanks to amazing activists in each and every generation, we've abolished slavery and segregation, we're actually working on providing women the rights they should have had in the first place, and we're more environmentally and socially conscious than ever before. So here's to everyone willing to stand up for what they believe in and speak out against corruption and oppression.

GREATEST GENERATION ACTIVISTS

RACHEL CARSON
Born: May 27, 1907
Known For: Environmental Activism, Author of *Silent Spring*

THURGOOD MARSHALL
Born: July 2, 1908
Known For: Civil Rights Activism, *Brown v. Board of Education*, First African American Supreme Court Justice

SILENT GENERATION ACTIVISTS

MARTIN LUTHER KING JR.
Born: January 15, 1929
Known For: Civil Rights Activism,
March on Washington for Jobs
and Freedom, "I Have a Dream"

GLORIA STEINEM
Born: March 25, 1934
Known For: Women's Rights
Activism, Anti–Vietnam War
Protests, Civil Rights Activism,
Human Rights Activism,
Fight for Peace

JANE GOODALL
Born: April 3, 1934
Known For: Environmental
Activism, Animal Rights Activism

JOHN LEWIS
Born: February 21, 1940
Known For: Civil Rights
Movement Leadership, U.S.
Representative for Georgia's
5th Congressional District
(1987–present)

JOAN BAEZ
Born: January 9, 1941
Known For: Civil Rights Activism,
Anti–Vietnam War Protestor,
Human Rights Activism,
LGBTQA Rights Activism

BABY BOOMER ACTIVISTS

ELLEN DEGENERES
Born: January 26, 1958
Known For: LGBTQA
Rights Activism, AIDS Awareness
Activism, Animal Rights Activism,
Environmental Activism, Human
Rights Activism

EARVIN "MAGIC" JOHNSON JR.
Born: August 14, 1959
Known For: HIV and AIDS
Awareness Activism

BARACK OBAMA
Born: August 4, 1961
Known For: First African
American President, Civil Rights
Activism, Human Rights Activism,
LGBTQA Rights Activism, Health
Care Reform

MICHELLE OBAMA
Born: January 17, 1964
Known For: Civil Rights Activism,
Human Rights Activism, Fight
Against Childhood Obesity,
LGBTQA Rights Activism

GEN X ACTIVISTS

TARANA BURKE
Born: September 12, 1973
Known For: Women's Rights
Activism, #MeToo Movement,
Civil Rights Activism, Human
Rights Activism

MILLENNIAL ACTIVISTS

SANDRA FLUKE
Born: April 17, 1981
Known For: Women's
Rights Activism

GEN Z ACTIVISTS

MALALA YOUSAFZIA
Born: July 12, 1997
Known For: Women's Rights
Activism, Fight for Access to
Education

EMMA GONZÁLEZ
Born: November 11, 1999
Known For: Gun Control
Activism, Human Rights
Activism

DAVID HOGG
Born: April 12, 2000
Known For: Gun Control
Activism, Human Rights
Activism

JAZZ JENNINGS
Born: October 6, 2000
Known For: Transgender
Rights Activism, LGBTQA
Activism

CAMERON KASKY
Born: November 11, 2000
Known For: Gun Control
Activism, Human Rights
Activism

SARAH CHADWICK
Born: August 1, 2001
Known For: Gun Control
Activism, Human Rights
Activism

GREATEST GENERATION:

WOMEN'S SUFFRAGE MOVEMENT

When: 1848 to 1920

Some Major Players: Carrie Chapman Catt, Elizabeth Cady Stanton, Ida B. Wells, Julia Ward Howe, Kate M. Gordon, Lucretia Mott, Lucy Stone, Marion Wallace Dunlop, Sojourner Truth, Susan B. Anthony

Some Major Events: 1848 Seneca Falls Convention, 1851 Woman's Rights Convention, White House Picketing by the National Woman's Party, Suffragette Marion Wallace Dunlop's 1909 Hunger Strike, 19th Amendment to the Constitution Ratified

Just the Facts: If you're paying attention to anything in this book, you'll notice this one pops onto the radar before the birth of the Greatest Generation. No, we didn't make a mistake (it's not worth figuring out how the postal service works to complain about it, trust us), it just took a long, long, long time for America to give women the right to vote. Like, from 1776 to 1920 long. Thanks to the blood, sweat, and tears of these ladies (not to mention some immaculate hats), women earned the right to vote with the ratification of the 19th Amendment in 1920. It's worth pointing out that only white women were allowed to vote—everyone else was stuck waiting on the gradual voting rights conveyor belt until 1966.

RISE AND FALL OF PROHIBITION

When: 1830s to 1933

Some Major Players: Billy Sunday, Carry Nation, Charles Grandison Finney, Elizabeth Cady Stanton, Dio Lewis, Frances Willard

Some Major Events: Second Great Awakening, Maine Passes 1851 Prohibition Law, Temperance Movement Gains Popularity, 18th Amendment to the Constitution Ratified, Rise of Bootlegging and Gang Violence, 21st Amendment to the Constitution Ratified

Just the Facts: Yes, believe it or not, Prohibition was an act of social activism. Shocker, we know. Temperance advocates had been pushing for America to sober up since the 1830s, and their distaste for the one thing that America loves almost as much as guns wasn't too unfounded. Alcohol was a big business, and money had a way of influencing politicians. Hard to believe in this day and age. But most temperance advocates were women who were more concerned with a man's soul than his bank account, believing they were saving the "moral fabric" of America, whatever that means. In a not-so-surprising turn of events, the "noble experiment" decided it didn't swing that way, paving the way for the rise of organized crime in the form of bootleggers. In 1933, America was over their experimental phase, and the 21st Amendment repealed Prohibition. Great Depression America breathed a sigh of relief and (legally) drowned their sorrows for the first time in almost 14 years.

SILENT GENERATION:

ENVIRONMENTAL CONSERVATION AND PROTECTION

When: 1930s to 1940s

Some Major Players: Franklin D. Roosevelt, Gifford Pinchot, Guy Stewart Callendar, Hugh

Bennett, Jay Norwood Darling, Marjory Stoneman Douglas

Some Major Events: Dusty Thirties, Black Blizzards, National Parks Service Reorganized, Civilian Conservation Corps Founded, Dedication of Everglades National Park, Soil Erosion Service Founded, Prairie States Forestry Project Founded, "The Artificial Production of Carbon Dioxide and Its Influence on Temperature" Published, Los Angeles Air Pollution Control District Founded

Just the Facts: Yeah, that's right, people cared about the environment before the '70s. While environmental preservation had been around since the late 19th century, the devastating impact of the Great American Dust Bowl left politicians, scientists, and farmers scrambling to put the American Dream back together again. The Industrial Revolution was finally starting to simmer down in the wake of economic downfall, leaving disease, pollution, and mass extinctions in its wake. Talk about Ghosts of Mass Production Past. Concerns over the way America handled its natural resources (spoiler alert: very poorly) led to the protection of national parks and the founding of environmental groups left and right in a desperate attempt to protect what little pieces of American wilderness remained. Now, don't get us wrong, this sudden concern for the environment—and the first evidence of climate change—didn't alter most of the world's day-to-day life (we're looking at you, asbestos), but we had to start somewhere.

THE LABOR MOVEMENT

When: 1930s to 1940s

Some Major Players: Arthur Goldberg, George Meany, John L. Lewis, Philip Murray, Samuel Gompers, Walter Reuther, William Green

Some Major Events: Workingmen's Parties, American Federation of Labor (AFL) Founded, the Great Depression, Roosevelt's New Deal, National Industrial Recovery Act Passed, Committee for Industrial Organization (CIO) Founded, Fair Labor Standards Act (FLSA), Flint Sit-Down Strike of 1936–37

Just the Facts: Let's be real, no one is really a fan of working a 40-hour work week, or making minimum wage, but you know what's worse than that? Not having either. With the wave of underemployment following the Stock Market Crash of 1929, the labor movement gained its first real foothold in American politics. This led to the passing of the Fair Labor Standards Act (you know, the one that means you don't have to work 60 hours a week) and collective bargaining strategies that gave workers the power of the masses. You try arguing against a veritable mob of workers. We dare you. The labor movement is a much larger slice of history than just the Great Depression, with origins back to before the founding of America, but the advances they pushed forward for workers' rights in the '30s and '40s are still being enjoyed today. So next time you're on your only 10-minute break for the day, hold up your phone in honor of the labor movement—the only reason you're not working an 18-hour shift.

BABY BOOMERS:

CIVIL RIGHTS MOVEMENT
When: 1955 to 1968
Some Major Players: Dr. Martin Luther King Jr., Rosa Parks, Malcolm X, Bayard Rustin, John

Lewis, Hosea Williams, Gloria Richardson, Roy Wilkins, Angela Davis

Some Major Events: March on Washington for Jobs and Freedom, Boycott of the Montgomery Bus System, Little Rock Nine, Civil Rights Act of 1957, Civil Rights Act of 1964, Voting Rights Act of 1965, Fair Housing Act of 1968

Just the Facts: The end of segregation, the beginning of equal employment, and the end of literacy tests at the polls were only a few of the fights won thanks to the civil rights movement. After a long, hard struggle, these activism giants took down the old system and paved the way for future generations to speak up and stand out. No jokes here; these guys were the real deal.

WOMEN'S RIGHTS (ERA)

When: 1970 to 1979

Some Major Players: Gloria Steinem, Robin Morgan, Ruth Bader Ginsburg, Betty Friedan, Angela Davis, Coretta Scott King

Some Major Events: Women's Strike for Equality, Reed v. Reed, Eisenstadt v. Baird, Roe v. Wade, National Advisory Committee for Women, Title IX

Just the Facts: The fight for equal pay, freedom from harassment, and body autonomy all got their foot in the door thanks to these killer ladies. Far from the damsel-in-distress stereotype, these wonder women of the '70s distressed leaders everywhere, spoke out against sexism and oppression, and gave new meaning to the phrase "fight like a girl."

ANTI–VIETNAM WAR MOVEMENT
When: 1963 to 1973
Some Major Players: Jane Fonda, Muhammad Ali, Joan Baez, Abbie Hoffman, Fannie Lou Hamer, Noam Chomsky
Some Major Events: School "Teach-Ins," Washington Protests, Kent State Massacre, U.S. Cancels Involvement in Southeast Asia
Just the Facts: Disillusioned hippies or brilliant protesters? Why not both! With anti-war activists ranging from college students and draft dodgers to world-renowned athletes and civil rights activists, the anti–Vietnam War demonstrations spelled the end of the United States' involvement in Southeast Asia. With somewhat organized marches, educational

"teach-ins" at local colleges, and a quasi-strategic offensive that set Washington on edge, this movement has been hailed as one of the most successful youth protests in history.

THE STONEWALL RIOTS
When: June 28, 1969
Some Major Players: Marsha P. Johnson, Sylvia Rivera, Raymond Castro, Martin Boyce, Virginia Apuzzo, Danny Garvin, Jerry Hoose, Thomas Lanigan-Schmidt, Dick Leitsch, John O'Brien, Seymour Pine, Yvonne Ritter, Fred Sargeant
Some Major Events: Stonewall Inn Police Raid, Stonewall Riots, Gay Liberation Front, Gay Pride
Just the Facts: The Stonewall Inn in Manhattan's Greenwich Village was anything but cozy the night the Stonewall Riots took place. This underground bar, funded by the mafia and packed full of members of the LGBTQA community, became the center of the gay pride movement thanks to a poorly timed police raid. After infiltrating the bar and forcing the patrons onto the street, police forces were met with resistant drag queens swinging handbags

and rowdy crowds cheering, "Gay pride!" The Stonewall Riots sparked a revolution across America that would eventually lead to the legalization of same-sex marriage in 2015. Stay fabulous, you kings and queens of LGBTQA rights.

MILLENNIALS:

MARRIAGE EQUALITY

When: 2004 to 2015

Some Major Players: Barack Obama, Evan Wolfson, Ruth Bader Ginsburg, Stephen Breyer, Sonia Sotomayor, Elena Kagan

Some Major Events: Decriminalization of Same-Sex Sexual Intercourse in All 50 States, Massachusetts Is the First State to Allow Same-Sex Marriage, Canada Legalizes Same-Sex Marriage, Goodridge v. Department of Public Health, United States v. Windsor, Obergefell v. Hodges, Same-Sex Marriage Legalized in All 50 States

Just the Facts: The fight for gay rights didn't start with millennials, but the largest victory in the LGBTQA community was won during their lifetime, with a hefty assist from Gen X, of course. The minute this generation made it to the polls they started handing in rainbow ballots, with Massachusetts becoming the first state to legalize same-sex marriage in 2004. After dozens of legal battles and a semi-united social media campaign that spanned 11 years, same-sex marriage was legalized across the United States in 2015. The Stonewall trailblazers would have been proud.

WOMEN'S MARCH

When: January 21 to 22, 2017

Some Major Players: Angela Davis, Gloria Steinem, Vanessa Wruble, Tamika D. Mallory, Carmen Perez, Linda Sarsour, Bob Bland, Harry Belafonte, LaDonna Harris, Dolores Huerta, Sophie Cruz

Some Major Events: Pussyhat Project, Women's March on Washington

Just the Facts: The Women's March took place the day after President Donald Trump's inauguration, with sister protests in 194 locations across 84 countries and an estimated five million participants worldwide. Sporting pink "pussyhats" and speaking out against violence, hate, and racism, the Women's March went down in history as one of the largest protests to ever grace the National Mall—drawing a crowd larger than the inauguration the day before. It was also one of the most peaceful protests in American history; not a single protester was arrested. Talk about a stunning display against hate.

#METOO
When: 2006 to Present
Some Major Players: Tarana Burke, Alyssa Milano
Some Major Events: MySpace Campaign, Social Media Campaign, Larry Nassar Allegations and Sentencing, Harvey Weinstein Allegations and Arrest, Bill Cosby Allegations and Sentencing, ME TOO Congress Act
Just the Facts: First started in 2006 as a way to show support for sexual assault victims, the #MeToo movement grew to encompass all sexual

BOOMER:

When you have people like Kanye West and Kim Kardashian as the spokespeople for your generation, I worry.

MILLENNIAL:

I know, if only we had figures like Bill Cosby to turn to.

assault and sexual misconduct claims, calling for policy reform and accountability for everyone from celebrities like Bill Cosby and Harvey Weinstein to politicians across the board. The movement started trending on social media as people encouraged anyone who had experienced sexual assault to simply post the hashtag. After hundreds of thousands of posts, #MeToo became synonymous with the unacceptable number of sexual assaults per year, as well as a rallying cry for change.

GEN Z:

MARCH FOR OUR LIVES

When: February 14 to March 24, 2018

Some Major Players: Emma Gonzálaz, Cameron Kasky, Alex Wind, David Hogg, Delaney Tarr, Sarah Chadwick, Jaclyn Corin, Ryan Deitsch, Aalayah Eastmond, Samantha Fuentes, Naomi Wadler

Some Major Events: The Marjory Stoneman Douglas High School Shooting, Never Again MSD, Enough! National School Walkout, March for Our

Lives, Marjory Stoneman Douglas High School
Public Safety Act

Just the Facts: The 2018 Marjory Stoneman
Douglas High School Shooting was one of the
deadliest school shootings in United States
history, with 17 students and staff members
killed and another 17 wounded. The survivors of
the attack stood up for themselves and for gun
restrictions, organizing the March for Our Lives
campaign for the one-month anniversary of the
shooting. With children as young as 10 years
old speaking at the event and sister marches
around the world boasting a total attendance
of over two million worldwide, the March for
Our Lives movement marked the largest youth
protest since the anti–Vietnam War movement.
Responsible for the founding of Never Again
MSD, a group whose goal is to prevent future
school shootings, these incredible students set
the pace for Gen Z's political involvement and
continue to fight for school safety.

BOOMER:

You are so obsessed with internet fame you don't stop to consider reality.

MILLENNIAL:

At least the cinnamon
challenge is less likely to
kill me than the pesticides
you put in our food.

CO₂ LATE

TIME FOR everyone's favorite topic: climate change. From melting ice caps to monster hurricanes, climate change is at the front of many political debates, news stories, and Facebook posts. And, surprisingly enough, this one doesn't get pinned on the millennials. Most rhetoric points fingers at baby boomers, blaming them for everything from increased global carbon emissions to the end of the world as we know it. That's a little harsh.

If we're being honest, boomers and boomer-run megacorporations didn't help the climate crisis, and some of the boomers in the political sphere are definitely a roadblock to change, but blaming the environmental crisis on just one generation is casting too small of a net.

We could easily go back through the Industrial Revolution and whittle out a nice chunk of responsibility for every generation since the 18th century, but that's a whole lot of effort and, honestly, outside the scope of a handbook. Go Google the 1850s or read anything from Charles

Dickens that isn't *A Christmas Carol*. Or don't, we're not the boss of you. If we were we'd only pay in experience.

But while the boomers are busy taking the blame for the fall of humanity, millennials are out in force for the environment. In a survey of over 31,000 millennials, climate change ranked as their top political policy concern, beating out international affairs and large-scale conflict. Take that, war.

BOOMER:

I'm worried I'll never meet my grandchildren.

MILLENNIAL:

I'm worried there won't be a planet left for mine.

Surprisingly enough, though, millennials rank worse than boomers when it comes to at-home recycling, and about half of baby boomers ranked climate change as their top policy concern. It seems while the boomers in the political sphere bicker about whether or not the environment is in their job description, the environmentally forward-thinking ones have decided to step in. Whether from misplaced guilt or a general love of nature, retired baby boomers are trading golfing and cruises for environmental sustainability, and there has been a marked increase in participation in local green groups.

Looks like the boomers are doing something right, after all.

"

BOOMER:

My generation is spending
our retirement cleaning
up the planet.

MILLENNIAL:

Worried about the karma
from all those Styrofoam cups
you dumped in the ocean?

"

This doesn't mean that millennials aren't doing their part for the planet—far from it—but millennials' focus strays from the small-scale factors of climate change and falls on kicking corporate waste right in the profits. It seems that the generation that grew up on documentaries about the environmental impact of corporations on local communities wants to take down the big guns, not hem and haw over an extra plastic bag at the grocery store.

Not only does this hip generation push for environmental responsibility on a large scale, but their shopping carts reflect their dedication. Studies show that these broke buyers are willing to shell out for sustainability. Millennials put the environmental impact of the companies they shop with as their number one priority and are willing to pay big bucks for things like sustainable packaging and business transparency, not to mention reusable straws. Companies focused on sustainability flourish, while big corporations are killed by the dreaded millennial.

It seems that unlike baby boomers, millennials put their money where their values are.

> "

BOOMER:

You're killing the economy!

MILLENNIAL:

It is to us what the
environment was to you.

HEY ALEXA, DEFINE TECHNOLOGICAL DEPENDENCE

LET'S PREFACE this one by saying yes, baby boomers have lived through the same technological shifts as millennials, because that's how the flow of time works. But for millennials, technology has never been stable. Ever since they could type in a web page address or wait for the dial-up tone, millennials have been on the cusp of the latest technological advances the minute they came off the proverbial press. They can still remember the days when you had to choose between making a phone call and surfing the web, when VHS tapes were the go-to in-home viewing technology, and Yahoo! was actually a popular search platform. For many of them, past technology is replaced by the latest gadget almost as soon as they grow accustomed to it. Old technology could mean anything from a flip phone to the iPhone 6, and with constantly updating websites, apps, and the fact that Facebook Messenger keeps changing its layout in spite of what anyone wants, millennials are at the mercy of their technological overlords. No wonder this generation has commitment issues.

"

BOOMER:

You act like you expect to change the world through a Facebook post.

MILLENNIAL:

At least I don't try and run the government through Twitter.

"

BOOMER:

Why are you so
obsessed with selfies?

MILLENNIAL:

Since you chose tax cuts
over health care, Instagram
is the only therapy we
can afford.

In true ironic fashion, the generation that is most concerned about natural living and environmental protection is also the most digitally connected. All thanks to the hellhole that is social media. Social media has taken hold of humankind quicker than almost any trend in history. If you think about it, even bathing regularly took a couple centuries to catch on in Europe. From MySpace in the early 2000s to Vine's six-second videos in 2013, being able to keep up with everything your friends and family are doing on a real-time basis has always been there for millennials. And people wonder why they're so impatient. When baby boomers were growing up, the easiest way to contact someone was to write them a letter. Or call them on a home phone, but there was no guarantee that they were actually going to be home to take the call. And until the answering machine rose to popularity in 1984, they would have no idea who called them without checking their phone records, which explains why serial killers were all the rage in the '70s.

This contact isn't necessarily a bad thing. After all, it allows almost anyone to access a network of knowledge larger than any that has ever existed. The fact that it's used to share cat pictures is neither here nor there. Take that, Library of Alexandria.

"

BOOMER:

You're too reliant on technology, you never read anymore!

MILLENNIAL:

Remember this moment
the next time you need me
to restart your router.

But recent studies have found that millennials are more likely to have mood disorders than the generations that came before them. And for being the so-called "laziest generation," the amount of time millennials spend "stunting" on social media is stunning. So why isn't "social media is destroying your self-esteem" trending on Twitter? Mainly because that's a 39-character hashtag, but that's not the point. It's mostly because social media is all so new. The first recognizable social media site was Six Degrees, started in 1997. It allowed users to create their own profile and connect with other people on the platform. From that point social media took off, with MySpace popularizing celebrity pages in 2003 and Facebook opening to the public in 2006. Before the youngest millennial was out of high school, social media was at the forefront of their world. While boomers struggled to turn on their computer, millennials grew up in a world where information could be spread to thousands of people in under three seconds with just one re-blog.

With likes, loves, and laughter pouring in on a daily basis, people should feel more connected to their friends and family than ever before. But for every yeet, plank, and Ice Bucket Challenge, there's a dark side to the web. Cyberbullying and internet stalking threaten children as young as middle school students, and the spike in suicide rates across all age groups gives even the most sarcastic Redditor pause.

Sure, social media and technology have opened the doors for millions of entrepreneurial careers, but with this instant transmission of communication and knowledge comes the worst social skills known to mankind. And we don't mean congress. In a recent study, 68% of millennials surveyed say they actively avoid face-to-face conversation. Sure, 80% of that total number were more than willing to text or email someone, but the idea of having a human conversation sent them into a panic. And they're worried it's holding them back from going from minimum wage to less than minimum wage.

"

BOOMER:

You understand that social media is not reality, right?

MILLENNIAL:

It seems far more real
than managing to leave
college debt-free.

That's not to say baby boomers haven't found their place in the Minion memes on Facebook and the comments section of the *Times*, but the millennials' social sphere extends to millions of people every second of the day. That could explain why they're all so obsessed with bath bombs. So baby boomers' jokes about millennials being attached to their phones at the hip (or the thumb) aren't that off the mark. But many millennials are unable to disconnect from their online social life for fear that it will disappear entirely. With more millennials moving away from friends and families and into urban centers to find jobs, a number of millennials are left with a choice between spending their time looking for new memes on iFunny or facing the actual loneliness of modern society.

That's not depressing at all.

BOOMER:

Every generation's kids blame their parents for their problems. Deal with it.

MILLENNIAL:

I'm sure my kids would blame me for something someday. Lucky for me, I can't afford to have them.

MILLENNIALS ARE RUINING THE REPOPULATION INDUSTRY

LET'S FACE IT, millennials just aren't getting married as fast as statisticians (or their grandmothers) think they should be, and they're waiting even longer to have kids. The average millennial puts off marriage until they're well into their 20s, in some cases waiting to get hitched until their mid-30s. This drop in the number of marriages and a rise in the number of couples putting off having kids has caused what population experts call a "baby bust": the exact opposite of the population spike that brought us the baby boomers.

That's good, right? The world might not survive another baby boomer generation. But millennials may be able to blame their marital cold feet on the baby boomers.

66

BOOMER:

Your generation has ruined
the sanctity of marriage.

MILLENNIAL:

And your generation's 50%
divorce rate hasn't?

Baby boomers got hitched slightly later than their parents, but the real hit to the Millennial Marriage Mind-Set (clickbait title, anyone?) has nothing to do with when boomers got married: it's when they get divorced. With the national divorce rate hovering at around 50% while millennials were growing up, it's no wonder that the next generation is jaded about the idea of the ideal American couple. With the spike in the number of divorces among baby boomers preparing for retirement (colloquially known as "gray divorces"), the aftereffects of a generation that stayed together "for the good of the kids" is a bit obvious.

Millennials are hesitant when it comes to long-term relationships, and with good reason: you want to make sure you really like the person you're going to split that $19 avocado toast with for the rest of your life! In all seriousness, millennials spend more time getting to know their life partners than past generations, and some are even forgoing the marriage part of the deal entirely, instead raising a family with their live-in significant other without worrying about all of the paperwork that goes along with it.

Millennials are hypersensitive to the cost of raising a child today, with daycare costs alone exceeding $1,200 per month per child in some states. Having a kid is like investing in a Ferrari: it's easier to look at pictures of someone else's than to pay for your own.

Recent polling shows that millennials aren't against the idea of having kids or getting married, they just want to be financially secure before taking on the care of another human life, and they want to make sure they have a loving, supportive partner before making that kind of commitment. Kind of sweet, if you think about it.

BOOMER:

If you can't look someone in the eye when you're talking to them, you'll never be able to build anything substantial.

MILLENNIAL:

Did you look Mom in the eye when you swore you'd be with her forever?

DIVORCING THE DIVORCE RATE

GET READY to add another American institution to the list of things millennials have killed. And no, we're not talking about mayonnaise (though honestly it was time for mayo to die). A study carried out in the United States between 2006 and 2016 found that divorce rates are dropping at an incredible speed. With how fast millennials are ditching paper, it's no surprise that divorce papers are on the fast track to becoming a thing of the past. Overall, the average percentage of marriages that end in divorce has fallen by 18%, a record low for the modern era. America has held on to its 50% divorce rate harder than they've vise-gripped the second amendment or fried food; but unlike the death of the McDLT, this seems like the one statistic people are happy millennials are finally bringing down.

Part of the fall in divorce rates has something to do with how late millennials are getting married. While the success of the millennial marriage could be attributed to how relatively short their married lives have been, and how short their lives have been in general (though if the media were to use that measuring stick they'd be out of clickbait), their hesitation to tie the knot might be saving marriage entirely.

Studies show that living with your significant other before getting hitched can benefit your married life by acting like a kind of "trial run" of the relationship before it's formally on paper. Think of it as those AOL discs that populate thrift stores across the country, but longer-lasting. Millennials also take more time to "shop around" for their soul mates. With the popularity of Tinder, Match.com, and, yes, even FarmersOnly. com, millennials have the whole world ahead of them when it comes to finding Mr. or Mrs. Right, so why settle for less?

There are also perks to maturing before choosing your significant other. Scientists estimate that the human brain isn't fully developed until age 25, which means people who get hitched in a hurry might not be making the soundest decisions. Millennials who opt to wait for financial and job security before committing can also be saving themselves some of the biggest stress factors in a marriage, since financial concerns are among the top reasons for divorce. Millennials are also ruining the extramarital affair, with studies showing they're more fond of sleeping in than sleeping around. And with some millennials forgoing tying the knot entirely to become a common-law couple with their live-in love bug, divorce is falling farther behind than ever before. Take that, divorce court.

BOOMER:

I'm worried you're not going to be able to take care of your mother and me when we're old.

MILLENNIAL:

I get the sneaking suspicion that this is the first time you've ever thought of the world existing long enough for you to grow old in it.

THE
TWILIGHT
FEARS

AH, RETIREMENT, the motivating factor that gets most of America's workforce out of bed in the morning. Those not-so-far-off leisure years filled with golfing, cruises, and learning to knit. With baby boomers perched on the edge of retirement, it's no surprise the American pension system is starting to falter. Every day, 8,000 to 10,000 baby boomers hit the "nifty sixty" mark, becoming the largest generation to reach retirement age.

But like we said earlier, baby boomers aren't retiring just yet. Part of this is thanks to modern health care. With the projected average American life span extending far past 80 years old, and with baby boomers set to live longer than any generation before them—or even after them, if some accounts are to be believed—retirement is being pushed further and further back, and becoming something of an afterthought.

Not only is retirement no longer around the immediate corner for baby boomers, but it might also not be in the cards. With the American pension system crippled under its own moribund weight and a decade or more tacked on to the end of the average boomer's life span, personal and private retirement savings are becoming more of an issue than ever before.

Retirement as a government policy is a fairly new invention that arrived on the tail end of the Industrial Revolution and has only really been around for about two generations. Before that, people worked until they were physically unable to work anymore. As depressing as that sounds, we might be headed back toward that endless-work lifestyle. In 2018, the BBC went as far as to suggest that we may all be working late into our 90s and even into our 100s if humans devise more and more ways to keep from shuffling off this mortal coil.

While living well over a century is the stuff of science fiction, working well into our centenarian years (that's a Scrabble word for you) feels closer to a dystopia.

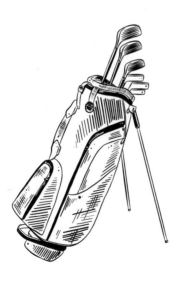

BOOMER:

We always just felt lucky
to have a job. We didn't
worry so much about
what the company did.

MILLENNIAL:

I guess when the future
is a swirling void of death
you wake up to what's
actually going on.

For workers who never cozied up to a business with a sizable pension program, or who ended up working low-income jobs, saving for retirement may have been entirely out of the question. Studies suggest that the average retiree should have at least $250,000 saved to maintain a comfortable lifestyle through their twilight years. But some reports suggest saving close to half a million dollars to combat the rising cost of health care. For many boomers, this just isn't possible.

So what now? The American pension system largely started to fall apart due to companies finding a cheaper way out of the Social Security payout system. And with the average cost of living steadily climbing, the pension system doesn't work half as well as it used to. Top financial advisers warn that there will be a drastic drop in payouts from the pension system as early as 2034. If changes don't happen soon, millennials may not be the only ones who can't afford a home. A 2016 survey found that 50% of homeless Americans were 50 years old or older, and the income levels of the older generation are steadily dipping below the poverty line.

So much for cruises.

CLOSING
REMARKS

"

BOOMER:

I look at your generation
and see no morals,
no backbone.

MILLENNIAL:

We didn't exactly have
great role models.

"

SO, BABY BOOMERS messed up a lot of things. Like a lot.

It's easy to look back on the entire baby boomer generation and lump them up into a sum of failures. Just like someone is going to do to millennials 40 years from now with another book that will not be half as funny as this one.

But for all their flaws, the baby boomers did help raise awareness about, and change, certain social ills. From the civil rights movement to passing the Clean Air Act, they may have not been perfect, but they did put some steps in place to try and make up for past mistakes. And with more baby boomers dedicating their retirement to fixing the environment, their contributions are far from finished. Does that bring back the rain forest or the West African black rhinoceros? Not really. But it does give them some semblance of a Shakespearean redemption arc. Exit baby boomer, pursued by malnourished polar bear.

There's an adage that has been passed down by cynical history teacher after cynical history teacher in an underfunded public school system for as long as people have been around: "People who don't learn from history are doomed to repeat it," followed by: "The one thing we can learn from history is that people don't learn from history."

Cheery, right?

Millennials have been given more technology, more knowledge, and more memes than any generation before them. And they have an entire generation that came before them as a wonderful example of how not to treat their fellow man, the planet, and fashion. Scientists estimate that if we keep going the way we're going with climate change, we might not be able to stop what we've already done. The world population is swelling to a size that might no longer be sustainable. Politics are more divided and volatile than they have been in decades. Whether they like it or not, millennials have been given a heavy burden to carry. We'd try and offer words of wisdom, but that's not really our speed.

But millennials are still just starting out. Who knows, they may actually invent a cool hover board before the Earth burns to a crisp. So long as they don't mess this up like the baby boomers did. Otherwise we'll have to add "everything" to the list of things millennials have killed.

No pressure.

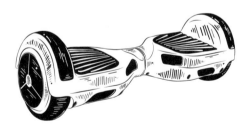

BOOMER:

I feel like your generation doesn't believe in anything.

MILLENNIAL:

No. We just don't think that beliefs and actions exist in separate dimensions.

ABOUT THE AUTHOR

Abigail F. Brown is an editor and writer whose native language is sarcasm. She spends too much money on avocado toast and is responsible for killing fabric softener, mayonnaise, and diamonds. She is still not sure if she's a millennial or Gen Z, even after writing this book, and at this point she's too embarrassed to ask.

ABOUT CIDER MILL PRESS BOOK PUBLISHERS

Good ideas ripen with time. From seed to harvest, Cider Mill Press brings fine reading, information, and entertainment together between the covers of its creatively crafted books. Our Cider Mill bears fruit twice a year, publishing a new crop of titles each spring and fall.

CIDER MILL PRESS

BOOK PUBLISHERS

"Where Good Books Are Ready for Press"

Visit us online at
www.cidermillpress.com
or write to us at
PO Box 454
12 Spring St.
Kennebunkport, Maine 04046